Nature's Children

RABBITS

Merebeth Switzer

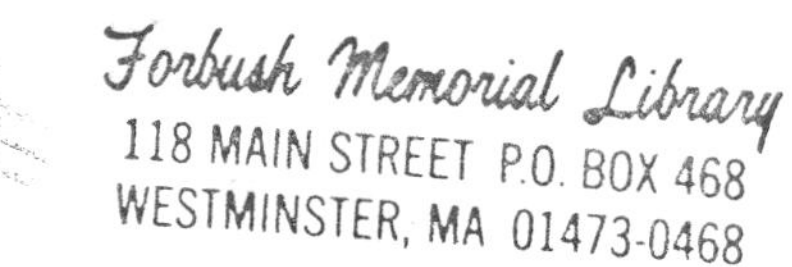

FACTS IN BRIEF

Classification of North American rabbits and hares

Class: *Mammalia* (mammals)
Order: *Lagomorpha* (''hare-shaped'' mammals)
Family: *Leporidae* (rabbit and hare family)
Genus: *Silvilagus* (rabbit); *Lepus* (hare)
Species: *Lepus americanus* (Snowshoe Hare); *Lepus arcticus* (Arctic Hare); several species of Cottontail and Jackrabbit.

World distribution. Cottontails, Snowshoe and Arctic hares and Jackrabbits are native to North America. Other types of rabbits and hares found are worldwide with the exception of Antarctica and the islands of southeast Asia.

Distinctive physical characteristics. Cottontail: fluffy white tail. Arctic Hare: very large; relatively short ears and legs; white coat at least in winter, some all year. Snowshoe Hare: very large well-furred hind feet; coat changes color—brown in summer, white in winter. Jackrabbit: huge ears and very long legs.

Published originally as
''Getting to Know . . . Nature's Children.''

This series is approved and recommended by the Federation of Ontario Naturalists.

This library reinforced edition is available exclusively from:

Sherman Turnpike, Danbury, Connecticut 06816

Contents

We all know something about rabbits and hares, even if it is only from watching or reading the adventures of Bugs Bunny or Peter Rabbit.

We know that they all have big ears and short fluffy tails and that they hop. And most of them seem to get into trouble by stealing garden vegetables.

You can probably think of many other story-book rabbits and hares. There is the March Hare in *Alice in Wonderland*, for instance, and that show-off who got taught a valuable lesson in Aesop's fable, *The Hare and the Tortoise*. And of course there is the Easter Bunny.

Certainly these story-book rabbits and hares are delightful and fascinating. But, they are no more fascinating than the real rabbits and hares that roam our fields and woodlands.

Average Size

Rabbit
38-45 cm (15-18 in)
0.6-1.8 kg (1½-4 lb)

Hare
45-75 cm (18-30 in)
1.8 kg (4 lb)

Rabbits or Hares: Who's Who?

Rabbits and hares are really quite different. But they look very much alike, and it is easy to get confused. In fact, it is so easy to get confused that some of them have been given the wrong names. For example, the Jackrabbit is actually a hare, and the Belgian Hare is actually a rabbit!

So how do you tell them apart? Well, generally, rabbits are much smaller than hares and have shorter legs and ears. But this is not always the case.

The only sure way to tell a rabbit from a hare is to get a look at the newborn babies. Baby hares are born with open eyes and a full covering of fur, and they can hop a few hours after birth. Baby rabbits are born helpless, blind, and with no fur on their bodies. It will be about a week before their eyes open and nearly another week before they are fully furred and hopping around.

Some rabbits and hares may be hard to tell apart, but there is no mistaking the Snowshoe Hare. Its huge, furry hind foot is more than one quarter the length of its body.

Rabbits, Rabbits Everywhere

Rabbits and hares are found all over the world except in Antarctica and the islands of southeast Asia. In some countries, such as Australia, there were no rabbits until fairly recent times. Early settlers brought some with them, and they quickly spread across the land.

In North America, rabbits and hares live in every type of wild area. Hares can live on the cold open tundra of the Arctic, in the hot desert, and high up in the Rocky Mountains. You can find rabbits in fields, swamps, marshes, woods, and even in the parks of big cities. If you live in the country or in a small town, you may very well have seen a rabbit or two in your garden.

All rabbits in North America are Cottontails, but there are several types of hares. The best

Where Cottontail Rabbits are found in North America.

Mother and baby Arctic Hare feast on the many kinds of plants that spring to life on the tundra during the short Arctic summer.

known are the Arctic Hare, the Snowshoe or Varying Hare and the Jackrabbit.

Home is Where You Find It

The hare does not have what we think of as a home. It simply uses whatever hiding place is available. This may be a clump of grass, a hollow log, or the low, overhanging branches of a fir tree. The hare will rest there all day with its body snuggled into the ground. This makes a shallow hollow called a form. A hare may use several forms, but it will usually have a favorite one that is "home."

In the winter, some hares may tunnel a short way into the snow and scratch out a cozy nook to shelter in.

Home to a Snowshoe Hare is often a low-hanging evergreen branch that shelters it from wind and falling snow.

Just as people around the world are different from each other, so are rabbits and hares. In Europe, rabbits build burrows and live in large underground communities called warrens. North American rabbits, on the other hand, follow the hare's example and use forms for sleeping. No one knows why North American rabbits do not dig burrows. It is not that they dislike them, because they do occasionally borrow someone else's—usually a woodchuck's or a skunk's.

Like many "rules" in nature, however, this one has an exception. One kind of Cottontail, the tiny Pygmy Rabbit that lives in the south-western United States, does dig its own burrow.

A nook in a snowbank might not suit everyone, but it's really quite comfortable—if you're a hare.

Getting Along with Each Other

Rabbits, Jackrabbits and Snowshoe Hares will usually live alone. Jackrabbits, in fact, seldom mix at all, even with their own kind. The others, however, are quite friendly with their close relatives and are sometimes seen feeding together or playing tag in a moonlit field.

On the other hand, the northern Snowshoe Hares and Arctic Hares are often found in large groups of over 100 animals. In these groups, aunts, uncles, brothers and sisters share the same feeding grounds and they will often play together in mock battles and chasing games.

Although both rabbits and hares are friendly towards their own kind, they are not friendly towards each other and you will rarely find rabbits and hares together in the wild.

Dinner-time

Rabbits and hares are most active at night. They spend the day in their forms snoozing and grooming themselves by licking their fur. Then, when it begins to get dark, they come out to look for food. It is safer for them to move around and feed when they cannot be seen.

Rabbits and hares are herbivores. This means they are animals that eat mostly plants. There is nothing a rabbit likes better than fresh greens, and it does not care where it finds them. No wonder farmers and gardeners sometimes think they are pests!

Rabbits and hares are active all year, always searching for food. During the northern winter, they feed on twigs, buds and the bark of certain trees. In the Arctic, where everything is covered by snow most of the time, the hares dig down to get buried moss and plants called lichen (pronounced *like'en*). Arctic Hares need up to half a kilogram (a pound) of food per day. Sometimes, in order to survive the Arctic winter, they will eat meat if they find it.

Better Than a Knife and Fork

Rabbits and hares have a set of very special front teeth to help them snip off plants and twigs for their dinner. Kangaroos can hop, and elephants have big ears, but no other animal has teeth quite like those of our friends the rabbit and hare.

Other animals—squirrels, for instance—have two big front upper teeth for cutting, just as rabbits and hares do. But rabbits and hares have an extra pair of smaller, very sharp front teeth just behind the big ones. This extra pair of cutting teeth is one of the main features that makes rabbits and hares different from all other animals.

Now that looks tender and juicy! What more could a hungry Desert Cottontail ask for?

Too fast for the photographer's camera to catch clearly, this super-hopper can still be identified by the white powder-puff tail that gives it its name.

Getting Around

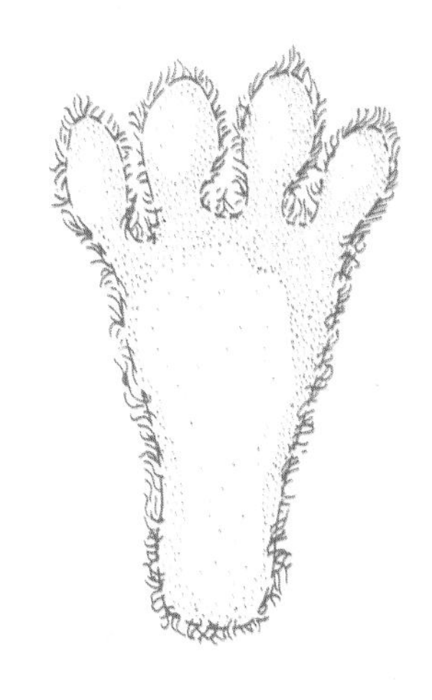

You know that rabbits and hares do not walk. But do you know what truly champion hoppers they are? If a Snowshoe Hare were as big as you, it would win all the gold medals in high jumping and broad jumping! This hare can jump four and a half metres (15 feet) straight up and can cover a distance about ten times its own length in one hop.

Snowshoe Hare's hind foot.

They are fast hoppers, too. Hares have been recorded at nearly 80 kilometres (50 miles) per hour over short distances. That is the speed cars go on the highways! Rabbits can reach about half that speed.

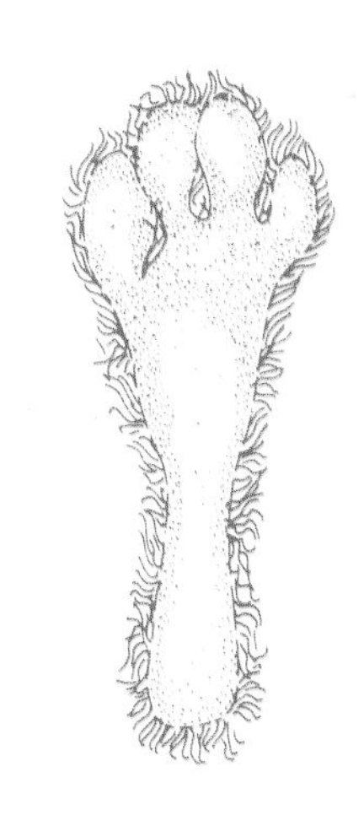

Jackrabbit's hind foot.

Snowshoe Hare tracks in snow.

How can a rabbit or hare jump that far, that high, and that fast? The secret is in its powerful back legs—they are huge and full of muscles. No wonder the hare in Aesop's fable did not worry about the tortoise in their race!

There is one type of rabbit that not only hops, it swims and even dives underwater. The Marsh or Swamp Rabbit is a type of Cottontail found in the southeastern United States. It gets its name because it likes to live in wet places. On very hot summer days, these rabbits are even seen lolling about in ponds or puddles to keep cool.

Although they move fast, rabbits and hares seldom go very far. Most, in fact, spend their entire lives within 400 metres (1300 feet) of their homes. The Jackrabbit may roam twice as far, however, and all will venture beyond their usual range if food is scarce. At mating season, as well, males may go courting outside their home range.

The hour after sunset is a favorite feeding time for bunnies.

Starting a Family

Baby rabbits and hares are born in the spring and summer, when the weather is warm enough for them to survive.

When the first signs of spring appear, the adult rabbits and hares begin their mating season. The males, called bucks, fight each other to decide who will father the young, while the female, the doe, waits nearby. Once this is settled, there may be an elaborate courting dance, with the buck chasing the doe and flagging his tail. The two may then dance around each other, play-box and leap high in the air. Sometimes they will groom each other by licking and nuzzling.

Rabbit Families

In southern Canada and in the northern United States, a doe rabbit may have three to five families, or litters, between March and September. In warmer climates she may have even more.

About four weeks after mating, the doe gets ready for the birth. She makes a nest in a shallow hole in the ground and carefully lines it with soft grasses and plants. She adds pieces of fur plucked from her own coat to make the nest extra warm for her babies. The nest is small and will only have room enough for the young babies, called kits.

Crouching over the nest, the doe gives birth to a litter of five or six babies. The kits are tiny—only about eight centimetres (3 inches) long. They cannot see and are completely helpless at this stage. Shortly after the birth, the mother allows her babies to nurse. Then,

These baby rabbits are probably about a week old. Their eyes are open, their furry coat is growing, and in a few days they will be up on their feet.

to protect the kits, she covers the nest with pieces of plants and she moves a distance away.

Keeping the Babies Safe.

During the first two weeks, the doe leaves the kits alone except when it is time for them to nurse. Even then, she approaches the nest in a careful zigzag pattern and leaps the last few feet in order not to leave a trail. In this way she keeps the babies' hiding place a secret from any animals that might be nearby.

In their nest, the kits are safe from most wild animals. But their open nursery can sometimes place them in danger at the hands of well-meaning people. A person who finds a nest often thinks that the mother has abandoned her babies. Nothing is further from the truth! The mother is very near, and she is looking after her family in the best possible way. Baby rabbits are difficult to care for, and they are safest if left alone.

There is nothing like a nice soft pillow!

Hare Families

Hares usually have fewer litters than rabbits do, and the litters are smaller in size. The mother hare behaves differently from the mother rabbit. She does not make a nest but simply stops at the nearest sheltered spot when she is ready to give birth. The chipmunk-sized babies, called leverets, are born covered in warm fur. Although they can see and are able to hop around a few hours after birth, the leverets still need their mother's care.

Sleeping is what baby Arctic Hares—like baby humans—do best.

The doe nurses her babies once a day under cover of darkness. This is her way of keeping their hiding spot safe from other animals. Like the rabbit, she leaves them alone the rest of the time but remains nearby, ready to lead enemies away. While their mother is gone, the babies huddle together in a warm brown heap for protection. Luckily they can soon scamper away to hide if any danger comes near.

The kits and leverets grow very quickly. Leverets are ready to leave the nest at three weeks, and the kits, who have more growing up to do, leave home at five or six weeks. Brothers and sisters may stay together for a few weeks before going their separate ways.

A baby Snowshoe Hare blends in so well with its surroundings that it is hard to tell where baby stops and surroundings begin.

Where Jackrabbits are found in North America.

Jackrabbits

Jackrabbits are actually very long-legged, long-eared hares. There are three main types of Jackrabbits: the Black-tailed Jackrabbit, the White-tailed Jackrabbit and the giant-eared Antelope Jackrabbit. You can guess how the first two got their names, but what about the third? The Antelope Jackrabbit is named for its white rump which looks like the rump of the Pronghorn or American "Antelope."

The Jackrabbit's huge ears are super scopes for sound, but they also serve another purpose: they help to keep the hares body cool in summer. The blood passes out into the ears and is cooled by breezes blowing over them. This helps to cool the whole body.

A Jackrabbit has the biggest ears for its size of any animal in the world.

The Snowshoe or Varying Hare

Where Snowshoe Hares are found in North America.

This hare lives in the forest. The name "snowshoe" refers to its very large hind feet. These act like built-in snowshoes and help the hare to move over deep snow without sinking up to its furry nose. They are even better than regular snowshoes because they are covered with thick, bristly fur that helps to keep the four big toes on each foot warm.

The Snowshoe or Varying Hare has a long, thick white coat in the winter to keep it warm and act as a disguise. In the spring it sheds this coat and grows a brown summer coat. The new hair is shorter and thinner and helps the hare to hide among the green and brown shadows of the forest. The change from white to brown takes nearly ten weeks, and the hare will look quite splotchy during this time.

Snowshoe Hares often create a year round trail or runway through heavy brush. The runways lead between favorite feeding and resting spots, and they are often borrowed by squirrels, porcupines, skunks, and other animals.

The Arctic Hare

The Arctic Hare is like the Snowshoe Hare, but is is nearly three times as big. A large body keeps warmer than a small one and takes longer to cool down in the cold. This hare also has unusually short ears and legs. The shorter ears and legs are closer to the hare's body and help to keep it warmer. They do not allow the body to cool the way the long legs and ears of the Jackrabbits do.

Where Arctic Hares are found in North America.

The Arctic Hare has a special fur coat made of two layers. Long silky fur lies over a layer of shorter woolly fur next to the body. The top layer keeps out the wind, and the bottom layer supplies warmth.

To save energy, the Arctic Hare spends much of its time sitting very still, like a statue. It tucks its tail and paws under its body and flattens

its ears along its back. It will sit this way sheltered behind rocks and snowdrifts or in the open facing into the wind. The wind presses the fur tightly against the hare's body, which helps to keep in the heat.

In the Southern part of their range, Arctic Hares grow a new brownish coat for summer. In the northern Arctic, however, summer is only a few weeks long, and hares living there do not change their white coats. This makes them very visible in summer against the brown tundra.

The short summer throughout the part of the world in which we find the Arctic Hare allows for only one litter of three to six babies each year. The leverets are greyish-brown at birth, which allows them to blend into their surroundings.

Their white coats make these northern Arctic Hares very easy to spot against the brown of the summer tundra.

A Dangerous Life

Rabbits and most hares have many babies each year. From one summer to the next, two pairs of rabbits could produce more than 160 children and 3000 grandchildren. Now that's a lot of rabbits!

If all the rabbits and hares survived, we would be knee-deep in bunnies. Why doesn't this happen? Small animals, such as rabbits, are very important to the balance of nature. They are dinner to foxes, owls, coyotes, weasels, lynx and others.

With so many animals looking for a meal, rabbits and hares must use all their wits to survive. They are always alert for danger, even when they take a short nap. Their huge ears catch every sound, and their constantly twitching nose sniffs the air for danger. Through the ground they feel the vibrations caused by people or other animals passing by.

Snowshoe Hare in the midst of changing from its white winter coat to its brown summer coat. The change helps protect the hare from its enemies by making it harder to see.

Survival Tricks

If an intruder moves near, rabbits and hares will flatten their ears and crouch close to the ground. If the danger comes nearer still, they flatten their body even further. In this position they look like a small rock.

When it appears that there is no escape from discovery, the rabbit or hare explodes from its crouch, leaping two to four and a half metres from a standing start. It then streaks away, hopping this way and that in a tricky zigzag pattern. This movement makes it very difficult for predators to follow.

Although rabbits and hares are usually silent creatures, all of them are able to let out a terrible, ear-piercing scream when they are captured or in serious danger. This often results in their being quickly dropped by their startled attacker.

A New Bunny Season

Young rabbits and hares just out on their own are in particular danger. They have not yet learned all their parents' escape tricks, and many unwary youngsters will fall prey to a watchful owl or fox.

The rabbit or hare that survives these first difficult weeks will soon be ready to start its own family. With luck, rabbits will live to one or two years of age, and hares may live for three or more years.

Words to Know

Buck Male rabbit or hare.

Burrow A hole dug in the ground by an animal for use as a home.

Courting dance A dance that always follows the same pattern and that is performed by rabbits and hares during the mating season.

Desert Hot dry area with few plants or trees.

Doe Female rabbit or hare.

Fall prey To be caught by an animal that hunts others for food.

Form Hollow in the ground made by a rabbit or hare snuggling in to sleep.

Grooming Brushing or cleaning hair or fur.

Herbivore Animal that eats mainly plants.

Kit Baby rabbit.

Leveret Baby hare.

Lichen A flowerless moss-like plant which grows on rocks and trees.

Litter Young animals born together.

Marsh Soft, wet land.

Mate To come together to produce young.

Mating season The time of year during which animals will mate.

Swamp Area where the ground is soaked with water.

Tundra Flat land in the Arctic where no trees grow.

Warren Piece of ground containing many rabbit burrows. European rabbits live in warrens.

INDEX

Cover Photo: William Lowry.

Photo Credits: Valan Photos: page 4 (Wayne Lankinen), 7, 16, 32, 35, 41, 43 (Stephen J. Krasemann), 8, 30, 37 (Brian Milne), 11 (François Morneau), 12 (Albert Kuhnigk), 19 (Kennon Cooke), 20 (Francis Lepine), 23 (J. D. Markou), 24 (Esther Schmidt), 27, 28, 45 (Harold V. Green); David R. Gray: 15, 39.

Printed and Bound in Italy by Lego SpA